At
with Lop

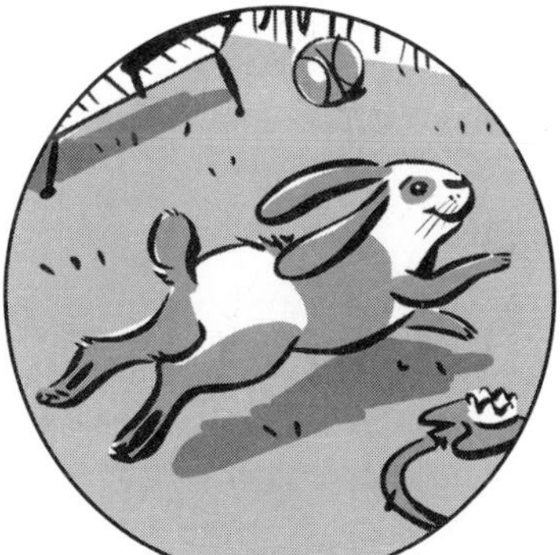

HOUGHTON MIFFLIN BOSTON

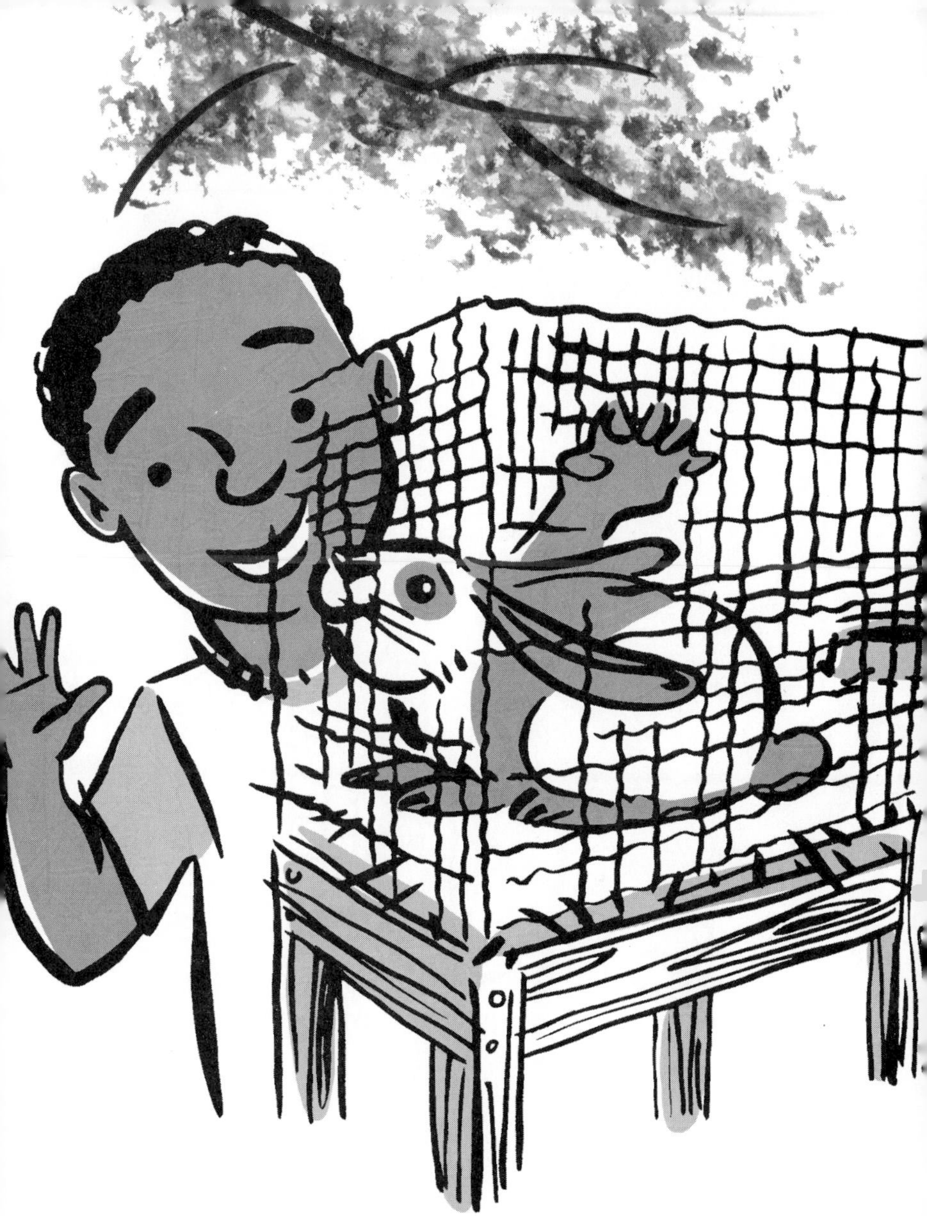

Sam has a pet rabbit named Lop.

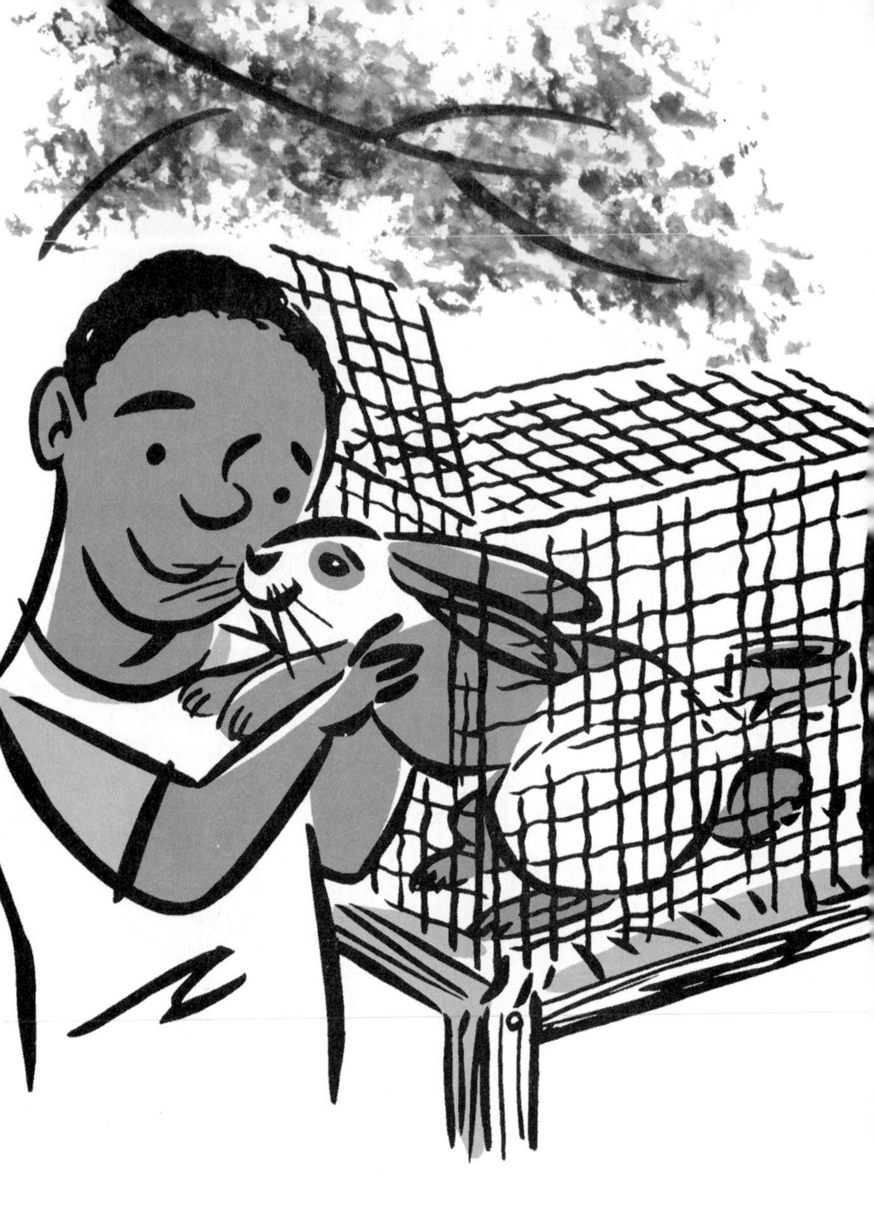

Sam lets Lop out of his cage for a while.

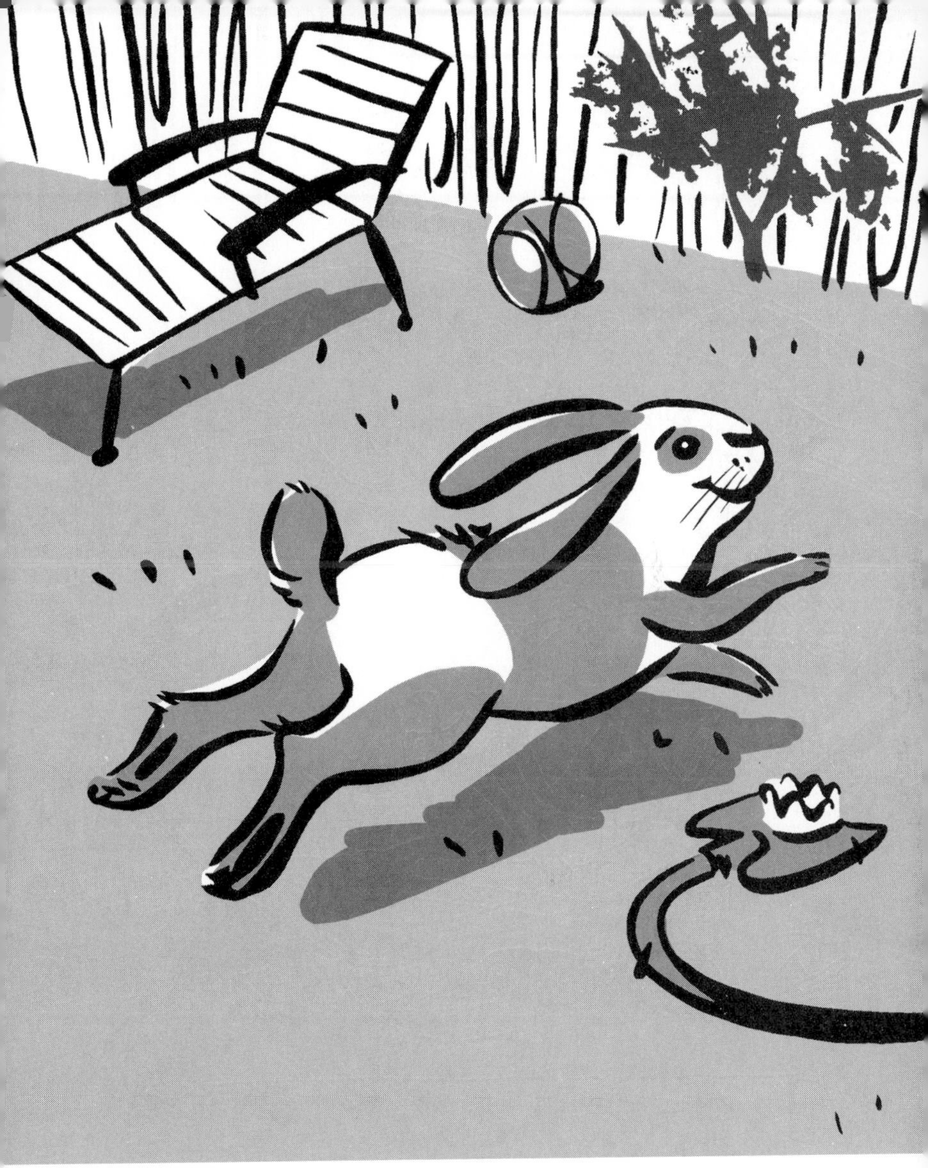

Lop hops to the fence.

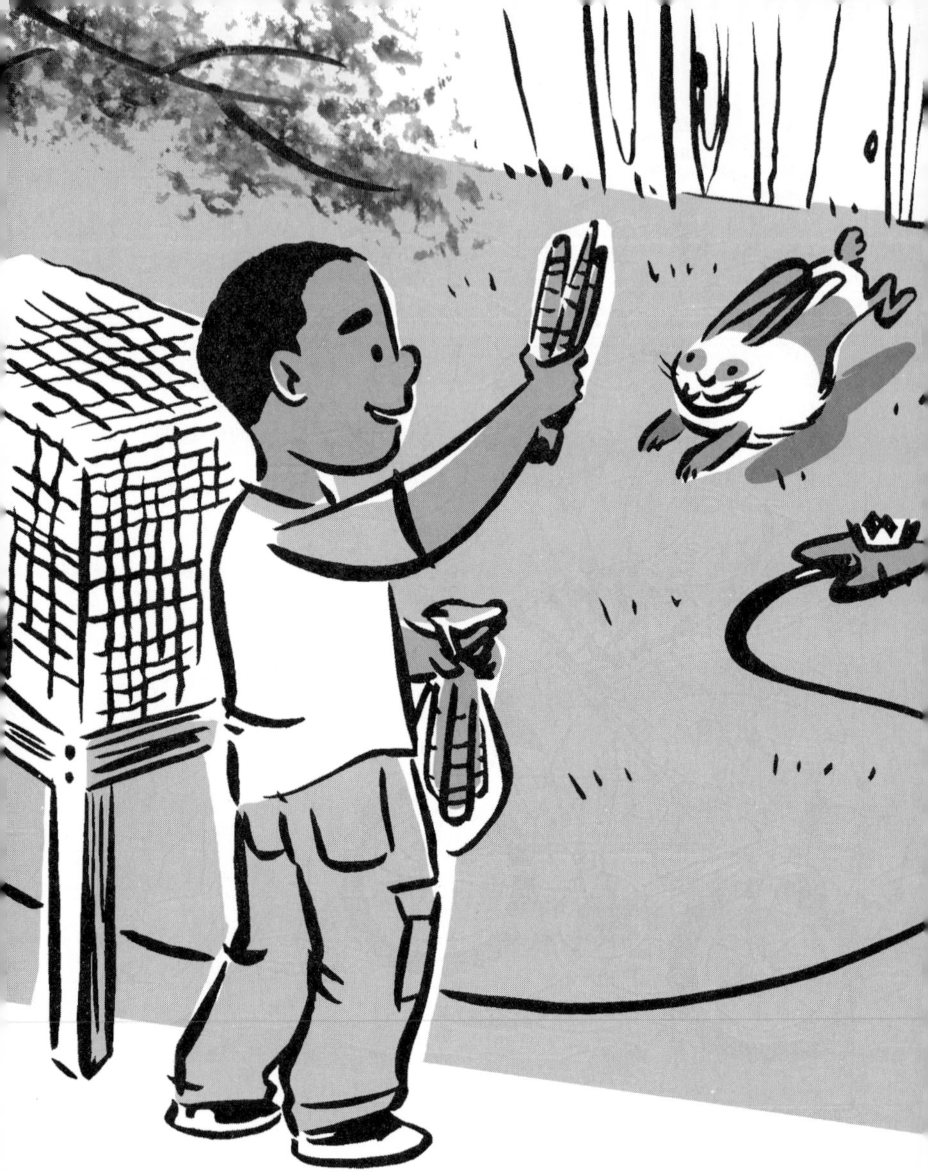

He hops back when Sam calls, "Carrots!"